EVIL ERNIE

YOUTH GONE WILD!

CREATED AND WRITTEN BY BRIAN PULIDO

ILLUSTRATED BY STEVEN HUGHES

CHAOS! COMICS

YOUTH GONE WILD!

Creator / Writer
BRIAN PULIDO

Illustrator
STEVEN HUGHES

Letterers
RONALD CRUZ & TIM ELDRED

Graphic Designer
MIKE FLIPPIN

President/Publisher	**Brian Pulido**
Vice President	**Francisca Pulido**
Office-Coordinator	**Kelly Jensen**
Graphic Designer	**Mike Flippin**
Chaos! Logo	**Leonardo Jimenez**
Evil Ernie Logo	**Legarretta & Flippin**
Founding Fathers	**Pulido & Hughes**

Published by Chaos! Comics, Inc, 7349 Via Paseo Del Sur, Suite 515-208 Scottsdale, AZ 85258. Chaos ! version. $9.95/$ 12.95 Canada Third Printing - Chaos! version.

DEDICATION:

TO MOM FOR LIGHTING THE FIRE
AND
DAD FOR POURING GASOLINE ON IT.
.....BRIAN PULIDO

TO MY SON, CHANCE (KID CHAOS).
.....STEVEN HUGHES

CHAPTER
ONE

1

CREATOR/WRITER
BRIAN
PULIDO

ARTIST
STEVEN
HUGHES

LETTERER
RONALD
CRUZ

3

9

13

CHAPTER TWO

2

EVIL ERNIE'S FANTASY:

SOMETIMES I *WORRY* ABOUT YOU, EVIL ERNIE...

YOU THINK *SMALL*. A MURDER HERE. A MURDER THERE.

WHAT WOULD YOU DO IF YOU HAD *GREAT POWER* ?

THE CURE THAT KILLS

CREATED AND WRITTEN BY:	PENCILLED AND INKED BY:	LETTERED BY:
BRIAN PULIDO	STEVEN HUGHES	RONALD CRUZ

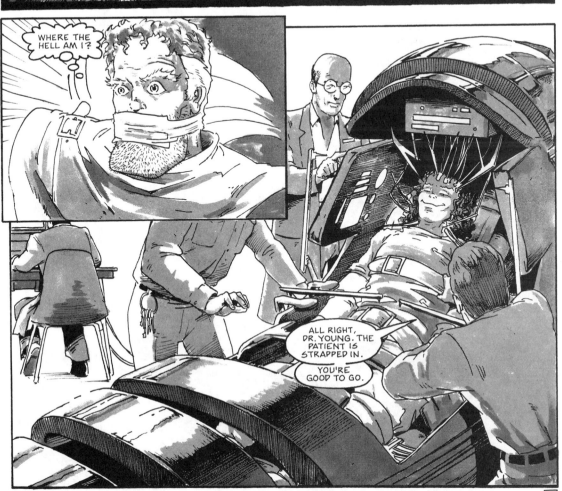

13

WHAT A BLAST! CREEP GOT *EXACTLY* WHAT HE DESERVED.

COULDN'T HAVE HAPPENED TO A *NICER* GUY.

...WE HAVE A BODY.

CAN YOU PICK IT UP, PRONTO?

GREAT.

I'M SERIOUS. ERNIE IS DEAD.

I'M SORRY.

SORRY?!

MY *REPUTATION* IS ON THE LINE!

WE'RE HAVING OFFICIALS OVER HERE TO *CELEBRATE* YOUR SUCCESS, DAMN IT!

THEY *FUNDED* NEUROTECH.

AS FAR AS I'M CONCERNED, IT WAS A *SUCCESS!* AND YOU BETTER GO ALONG WITH ME MARY.

NOW GET *OVER* HERE!

I'M LEAVING. I'LL CHECK IN LATER.

23

CHAPTER THREE

CREATED AND WRITTEN BY // PENCILLED AND INKED BY // LETTERED BY
BRIAN PULIDO // STEVEN HUGHES // RONALD CRUZ

2

14

CHAPTER FOUR

4

WHAT'S UP, DOCS?

Heh. Heh.

MAD LOVE AND MAYHEM

A PULIDO & HUGHES COMIC, BOY-EE!

CREATED & WRITTEN by BRIAN PULIDO   ILLUSTRATED by STEVEN HUGHES   LETTERED by TIM ELDRED

①

WHAT THE HELL IS THAT?!

MUST BE ONE'A THOSE THINGS!

SHOOT IT!!

⑨

GET IT
IN THE
HEAD!

BLAM

SUBURBIA.

THOUGH THE BULLET ONLY
GRAZES EVIL ERNIE'S HEAD,
THE GHOULS FEEL ITS
AGONIZING EFFECTS ON
THEIR MASTER.

ERNIE'S PAIN IS
THEIR PAIN.

BUT THE PAIN
SUBSIDES...

HIT IT IN THE
HEAD AGAIN!
IT DIDN'T
LIKE THAT!!

...AND IN SUBURBIA, THE MURDER
MARDI GRAS CONTINUES.

WITHOUT A *BRAIN*, ERNIE CAN'T CONTROL THE DEAD.

I THINK.

WHEN WE GET IN RANGE, THAT'S WHAT WE'RE AFTER.

GOT IT.

GO!

KILL!

YEAH, I'M A GOOD BOY!

TIRED, TOO.

14

INSIDE DR. MARY YOUNG'S HOME...

WE NEVER SHOULD HAVE TRUSTED STONE. THAT AMBITIOUS **FOOL!** WE'RE **RUINED!**

"A MENTAL PURIFICATION DEVICE." WHAT WERE WE **THINKING??**

GOD FORBID IT GETS OUT THAT YOU **APPROVED** THIS TEST!

YOU CAN KISS YOUR MERCEDES GOOD-BYE, AM I RIGHT?

ABSOLUTELY.

I SUGGEST DR. MARY YOUNG IS AT FAULT.

HER MACHINERY DID THE DEED.

I **LIKE** IT.

THEN IT'S SETTLED. DR. YOUNG TAKES THE BLAME.

YOU THINK I DIDN'T **HEAR** THAT? WHY DID MARY GET INVOLVED WITH YOU MANIPULATIVE BASTARDS?

WE DON'T EVEN KNOW IF SHE'S **ALIVE!**

WE SHOULD THROW YOU **OUT** WITH THOSE THINGS!

RIGHTEOUS IDEA!

I'M TEMPTED.

LADY DEATH?

INSIDE EVIL ERNIE'S MIND IS A NIGHTMARE NETHERWORLD OF HIS OWN MAKING WHERE ALL IS DEAD OR DYING. IT IS HIS SANCTUARY, THIS EVIL PLACE.

IT IS HIS FANTASY.

LADY DEATH!

(17)

THERE'S THE HEARSE. WHERE'S THE CREEP?

NOTHING IN HERE.

STAY SHARP. IT'S QUIET.

TOO QUIET.

GUESS THE GOOD GUYS LOST.

I'M GOING TO LOOK FOR A PHONE.

BE CAREFUL. HE COULD BE ANYWHERE!

HEAVY ARTILLERY. THAT'S WHAT WE NEED.

I WANTED TO HELP ERNIE. I DIDN'T KNOW HOW SEVERELY ABUSED HE WAS.

HIS PARENTS TWISTED HIM BEYOND ANYONE'S HELP.

BUT I LISTENED TO THEM. THEY SAID HE WAS WITHDRAWN.

IDEALISM.

THE DISEASE OF *IDIOTS*.

LINE'S DEAD.

I WONDER HOW BILLY, JUDY AND RICK ARE HOLDING UP.

PLEASE LET THEM BE ALL RIGH

IT WASN'T SUPPOSED TO TURN OUT THIS WAY.

I ONLY WANTED TO HELP.

I *HAVE* TO REACH MY FAMILY!

GOOD LORD, WHAT HAVE WE *CREATED?*

DAMN!

BLA

KN O_K!

KNOCK!

KNOCK!

KNOCK!

YOU BETTER ANSWER THE DOOR, ERNIE.

23

CHAPTER FIVE

2

I DID IT! I KILLED EVIL ERNIE!

IN SUBURBIA...

ERNIE'S PAIN IS THEIR PAIN!

ERNIE'S ARMY OF THE UNDEAD WRITHE IN AGONY!

GRRRRRR

GRRRR

IMPOSSIBLE!

NOT!

3

4

5

VISIT THE FAMILY!

THE PSYCHO-PLAGUE HAS GROWN STEADILY **WORSE**. MAJOR SECTIONS OF THE U.S. ARMY ARE **M.I.A.** IN THE STRICKEN AREA. EXPERTS, BATTLING AGAINST TIME, CANNOT FIND **REASON** OR **CURE** FOR THE PLAGUE.

PLAGUE
+CURE+

CHANNEL NEWS

KEEP DOORS AN WINDOWS **LOCKE** DO **NOT** VENTUR OUT. BE **WARNE** ANYWHERE IN THE TRI-STATE AR IS SUSCEPTIBLE TO THE **PSYCHO PLAGUE!**

IT HAS SPREAD THAT FAR, AND THERE IS **NO END** IN SIGHT. REPEATING: **MARTIAL LAW** DECLARED IN NEW JERSEY.

RICK, I'M SCARED!

MARY'S OK. I'M SURE.

WHERE'S MARY?

LET'S SETTLE DOWN FOR A MINUTE.

LISTEN—GO TO THE ROOF AND *HIDE.* DON'T COME DOWN, NO MATTER *WHAT.*

FORGET IT, MAN. WE'RE *STAYIN'.*

WE'LL *FIGHT.*

WE CAN'T TELL *WHO'S* COMING. IF IT'S MORE GHOULS, I SAY WE SACRI-FICE THE *KIDS.*

YOU GUTLESS *DWEEB!* DON'T EVEN *THINK* OF IT!

IF *ANYBODY* GOES, IT'S *YOU,* STONE!

CAN'T THIS CRATE GO ANY *FASTER?*

LOOK, I DON'T KNOW HOW TO *OPERATE* THAT THING BACK THERE. YOU BETTER CLAM UP AND KEEP READIN' THAT *MANUAL!*

WHAT THE HELL IS GOING *ON* OUT THERE?!

CAN'T SEE A *THING!*

STONE! COME BACK, YOU COWARD!

FOOLS! I'M NOT GOING TO DIE!

NO! NO!

HELP ME!

DO YOU KNOW WHO I AM, YOUNG MAN?!

YOU'RE IN DEEP TROUBLE!!

CRAC

NOT THEM! BYE-BYE!

KRAK!

15

17

19

23

THE END.

STEVEN HUGHES
SKETCHBOOK

CHAOS! ARCHIVES

ON THE FOLLOWING PAGES YOU
WILL FIND THUMBNAIL SKETCHES
FOR EVIL ERNIE #1 WHICH
FEATURE A DIFFERENT "DREAM PROBE"
SEQUENCE & A DIFFERENT
INTRODUCTION FOR LADY DEATH.

SNUFF SAID!

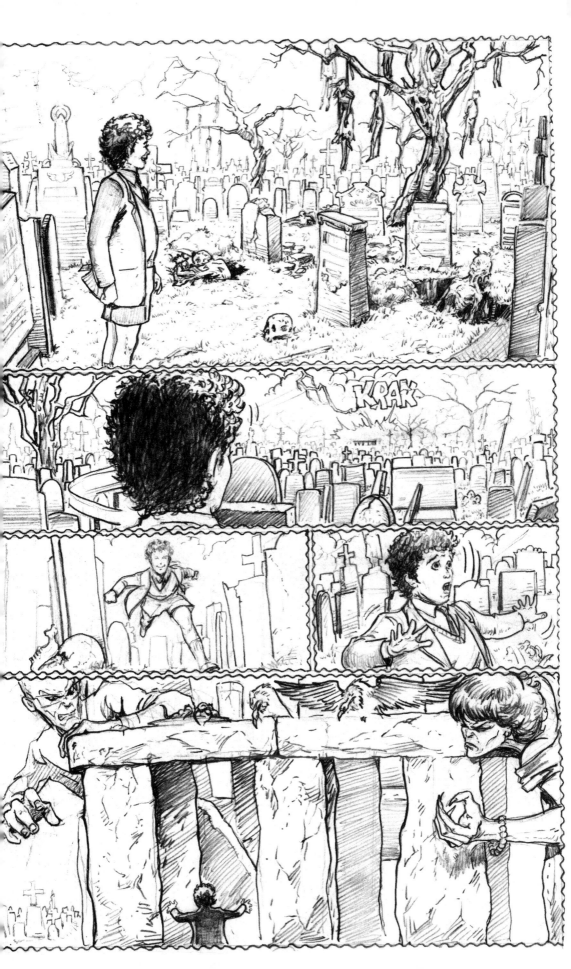